YOUR LIFE TEACHES YOU TO LIVE

5 Fingers For A Fist Of Power With Peace

By Doretta Lee

Printed in Victoria, BC, Canada.

ISBN: 978-1-4269-2717-1 (soft)
ISBN: 978-1-4269-2658-7 (hard)

Library of Congress Control Number: 2010902138

*Our mission is to efficiently provide the world's finest, most comprehensive book publishing
service, enabling every author to experience success. To find out how to publish your
book, your way, and have it available worldwide, visit us online at www.trafford.com*

Trafford rev. 4/5/2010

 www.trafford.com

North America & international
toll-free: 1 888 232 4444 (USA & Canada)
phone: 250 383 6864 ♦ fax: 812 355 4082

Thanks to everyone who contributed to the experiences in my life which gives me the confidence to write this book. Whether those experiences with you were good, bad or indifferent; I believe you and the affects of our acquaintance promoted me to a level of understanding that is priceless.

Thanks to you who have opened doors for my insights to be heard orally, read, viewed on the internet and any other Medias I am found on

Thanks to my close family and real friends, who have supported me with love gifts of money and genuine encouragement.

Contents

INTRODUCTION   ix

I.   THE NEED TO DESIRE   1

II.   THE EXCELLENCE OF ARROGANCE   13

III.   THE STUBBORN LIFE OF THE STRONG
      WILLED   25

IV.   THE INDEPENDENTLY LIBERATED   37

V.   THE HUMBLENESS OF PASSIVITY   49

VI.   5 FINGERS FOR A FIST OF POWER WITH
      PEACE   59

SUMMARY   71

CONCLUSION   75

ABOUT THE AUTHOR   85

INTRODUCTION

What prompted me to write this book was an email I received in July of 2009 inviting me to speak at an event in Austin, Texas. They reached out to me after viewing a You Tube video of me speaking at a Women's Conference in Connecticut in June of 2009. They felt I had something valuable to share at this event and informed me there would be an opportunity to distribute my work for purchase. I realized I had a lot of thoughts in my head I had never put on paper, CD or DVD. Given I had only a month to really prepare written material to display for this event, I began to shuffle through my pool of thoughts. My intentions are always to give a balanced perspective based on my personal experience, testimonies of others and knowledge acquired from other sources. I believe my experiences have a value worth sharing, so I am honored to have this opportunity to translate a few of them within this book.

This book is not gender bias and it is race, creed and color friendly. I try to keep a universal perspective in mind when writing because I refuse to be boxed into a class of writers based on my gender, religious beliefs, nationality or skin color. I believe everyone should have standards to live by but those standards will only govern the external representation of us. It is very possible to have something totally different going on inside our thoughts and feelings. My intentions are to help bring both the external and internal on one accord.

Some of us have been searching for answers to simplify our lives so we can have peace of mind. To our dismay, we have found the more we search the more complex life seems to be. There are many books on nearly every subject in question yet there seems to be only a short-lived satisfaction from the knowledge they present....from dieting to relationships. Even when we put the knowledge to use, we find ourselves being drawn back to some of the same situations we worked hard to get out of.

We try to do things within our power to improve our lives: moving to better neighborhoods, higher levels of education, changing our eating habits, meditation, group therapy, rigorous exercise and the list goes on. Many of the changes made our lives more complex though we were led to believe these changes would bring greater joy to our lives. The amount of effort and thought it took to apply those practices, made it impossible to keep up the application for long. This is why there are so many diet fads, relationship guru's and exercise programs but we need answers for the long haul not quick fixes.

In our quest to have a certain quality of life, we can lose the very essence of who we are. *"When who we are is over ridden by what we want then what we want becomes who we are"*. Instead of being loving, we are famous; instead of being giving we are rich; instead of being nurturing we are idolized. I believe it is possible to be famous, rich and admired without losing the essence of being loving, giving and nurturing. When we keep our essence in place as we gain a better quality of life, we leave an intangible inheritance to those we are close to. They will have an imprint in their hearts more valuable than any book of knowledge available.

My thinking behind the 5 Fingers For A Fist Of Power With Peace represents what taking our life into our own hands can be like. We can be powerful with peace when we take charge of whom we are and where we're going internally. The internal work is the foundation that will allow us to enjoy the external rewards we seek. When we see the importance of how all aspects of our lives work together to create the power we need not only to excel in the area we wish to excel but in the power to demand peace in our lives. Unfortunately, power and peace have to be fought for but the fight doesn't have to be physical or directed at anyone else. The fight is within ourselves to illustrate to others who we are and how we expect to be treated.

There is no need to apply force to get what you want because *"When who we are is over ridden by what we want then what we want becomes who we are"*. If you desire respect, you have to override the desire to be disrespectful, even to those who disrespect you. If a disrespectful action overrides your desire to be respected then you become "disrespect". Whatever you want to be has to override all negative reactions and responses that are designed to sabotage your objective. It's a process that won't happen overnight but it can and will happen if you put your energy into your positive image verses the negative draws that pull at us daily.

I am not a counselor, psychologist, psychiatrist or a licensed therapist. I don't claim to have coined the answers to all of life's complexities but the application to these observations has simplified my life in many areas. So I encourage you to at least give this information some serious attention. A very significant thing about what I am sharing is it won't cost you any additional money to apply this information....and that's the beginning of simplicity.

I. THE NEED TO DESIRE

- The Thumb

I love probing the dictionary for its interpretation of a word as well as other sources to compare my thoughts, others' opinions and shared definitions between those who created these resources.

Like a mad scientist, I sometimes go about trying to disprove their conclusion. I feel this is necessary in order not to fall into a robotic mindset. I don't believe you can ever exhaust research, there's always a chance those great minds before us missed something. So keep in mind the definitions I give in each chapter are based on my personal summary of all the information I've gathered.

The chapters are arranged in what I believe is a progressive order to finding simplicity in this complex society. When I think of simplicity I really am describing peace. Simplicity in itself is a matter of opinion. Simplicity to me and you could be very different but what makes it mutual is peace. At the end of the day, do you have peace in how you played the game? Are you satisfied with your efforts vs. did you win?

There are certain things in our life that are needs. We must have shelter, food, income, people, water, sleep, and clothing but sometimes it's not easy to get all of these needs met. It seems as if we are in a game and part of the game should come with being set up with needs. For instance, in the game Monopoly you start off with a certain amount of money and an object to move around the board. You need those items to participate in the game. Football requires a ball and an even amount of players on both sides; video games require a monitor, controls, a game cartridge and game box. When our needs are in place, we can proceed with life but the object of the game is to never run out of the needs or the resources to get them met.

Life can get confusing; there are many ideas about what needs are and what it takes to maintain those needs, our lives have become more complicated than necessary.

NEED:

Necessary supplies to sustain ones general well-being

DESIRE:

A strong expressed craving for things not immediately attainable

No matter where you live or who you are, there are certain things that are universally considered needs. Water, food and shelter are universal needs no matter what living creature you are. Animals and insects have a greater sense of what needs are than most of us who are capable of thinking in dimensions. I have created a list based on need and desire as I see it. I don't expect you to agree totally with the specifics of the two lists. The setup is mainly for the purpose of explaining the concept.

NEED		**DESIRE**	
SHELTER	Protection From The Elements	BRICK HOUSE	Dream House
WATER	Hydration	SWEET TEA	Favorite Drink of Choice
BREAD	Basic Food	STEAK	Higher Quality of Food
INCOME	Hand Out, Minimum Wage, Welfare	WEALTH	Money To Afford Extravagance
PEOPLE	Associates, Neighbors	SIGNIFICANT OTHERS	Spouse, Family Members, Friends

HEART	Necessary Organs To Live	COSMETICS	Implants, Reductions, Lifts
AIR	Oxygen For The Lungs	LOVE	Feelings Of Closeness
SLEEP	Rest To Rejuvenate	VACATION	Leisure, Relaxation

If we were to make a personal needs list, it might include some of the items on the desire list. Based on the dual list, there's a distinct difference in needs and desires but based on our lifestyle there's a thin line between the two. There are days that no matter how thirsty I am water alone don't seem to quench it but a big cold glass of sweet tea might. Even though the water served its basic purpose in hydrating me I didn't feel satisfied. Could it be that desires are based on emotion since they aren't necessities? Do our desires serve as a temporary emotional rush like a drug?

There's a drive in the universe towards desires that has all but eliminated the reality of what a need is. Most of us have been infected by the pressures of the society to put desires before needs. "Get your desires met and you'll be happy for life" Most desire can be coined in "Get Wealth".

Wealth is relevant to what your desires are....some base wealth on what their neighbors have (being able to keep up with the Jones') while others base wealth on being a millionaire. So the pursuit for happiness is geared toward obtaining a certain level of income. When we overlook the needs to get to the desire, there will be an imbalance. Putting need before desire is as essential as laying a foundation before building a house. I believe how well we understand what needs are will determine how satisfying the acquired desires will be. If we bypass a need to get to a desire, eventually there will be dissatisfaction with the desire. For instance, If we never consumed the water but only the sweet tea our kidneys and other filtering organs will be overworked and eventually need repaired or replaced.

I believe it is important to make sure needs are met prior to the equivalent desire. Identifying and satisfying needs gives us a greater appreciation for the desires. When we have clarified the difference between need and desire, we can keep a realistic attitude as we pursue the desires once the needs have been properly met.

I believe it is necessary to have desires. The Need To Desire is what keeps us progressively thinking. Progressive thinking is necessary to keep up with and ahead of the ever changing universe. To enjoy the quality of life, we must keep in mind meeting the needs prior to the desire will establish a firm foundation of thoughts and actions.

> *"Forsake the foolish, and live; and go*
> *in the way of understanding"*

5 Fingers For A Fist Of Power With Peace The Thumb - Imagine life without a thumb, you can accomplish many things but the stress and strain to hold onto something without it can be frustrating. The thumb simplifies our lives and this is what identifying needs verses desires should do. There is a power and peace in having your needs met because you have established structure by putting desires in their proper place.

HAPPILY EVER AFTER

One day a teen aged girl (we'll call Vaneese) noticed the happiness of a man and a woman as she walked to the park to meet her friends. She saw them occasionally in her neighborhood walking, laughing, smiling and holding hands; they looked like the ending of a great story. They had the look of "happily ever after" which reminded her of the fairy tales her mother once read to her as bed time stories. Vaneese loved the memories of those fairy tale stories. No matter what difficulty the characters faced in their lives it always ended up with a great ending of living happily ever after with the person they loved the perfect home and wonderful friends.

Even though her life wasn't difficult, she noticed her parents seemed to be at odds with each other a lot more than usual. The memories of fairy tales kept her believing the story between her parents would eventually end like all the stories read to her.

The arguments between her parents had much of the same content. Her father would say "I don't do the things you want because you don't do the things I need you to do for me". Her mother's response would be, " I don't do what you want because you don't give me what I need". Then they would list to each other what the needs were; the mother insisting she needed time away from the kids, attention, affection, a bigger house and for him to be more involved with the family issues. Her father's request was for peace and quiet, more home cooked meals, a newer car, a skinnier wife and her to be more social with his friends.

Vaneese thought about her mother's list of needs; it felt strange to her for her mother to want to spend time away from her children. She didn't really understand what affection and attention her mother wasn't getting since they were always telling each other they loved one another.

She laid in her bed at night thinking about what made people have problems with each other and what brought them back together to the "happily ever after" ending according to the fairy tales. As she went over in her head every fairy tale story she could remember she thought about what part of each story signified the difficult times were about to turn around. She rationalized if she could pin point those moments then she could help this real live fairy tale get to the beginning of the "happily ever after".

From looking at the couple in her neighborhood, she knew it was possible to live like the fairy tales ended.

One thing that puzzled Vaneese was how both her parents could be so unhappy when they had so much. They lived in an upscale neighborhood, both well accomplished in their career fields and respected by their peers. As she examined the fairy tales she realized there were a few things they all had in common. One person (usually a woman) would be in distress and the other (usually a man) would come to the rescue. The one rescued fell in love with the hero but found that the hero was more concerned about rescuing others than being in love. Because of his desire to be a hero all of the time, he was blinded to the love that he desperately needed to be really happy. In the fairy tales, the lady who fell in love with her hero grew weary of trying to win the heart of her hero and began to pull away. After a while, no matter how many times the hero rescued someone he didn't feel satisfied because he had no one he felt close enough to share his victories with. When those feelings of loneliness took over he suddenly realized what he was missing was a person who loved, respected and honored him. However, his pride and fear of rejection wouldn't allow him to ask for the love he needed. When confronted by friends who saw his unhappiness, he would deny his feelings and need for love. He felt giving in to the need for love would make him lose his credibility of being strong; while all along on the inside he was beginning to feel weaker and weaker.

The problem seemed to be the unwillingness of each character to recognize each other's need. They both were experiencing great desires being met in their lives but those desires could not be fully appreciated without the needs being met.

Vaneese had a great challenge ahead of her to bring the two people she loved the most to their "happily ever after". She decided to place herself in the picture by doing to them what they had been doing to each other. Vaneese began to express to her mother how she missed the fairy tale stories she read to her as a young child. The mother said she felt as a teenager those stories were no longer appropriate and that she should find time to read to herself. Her mother complained that Vaneese wasn't keeping her room as tidy as she'd been taught to do and she should focus more on doing what's needed around the house. Vaneese explained to her mother the amount of chores that were placed on her was stealing time away from her hanging out with her friends. They continued several minutes going back and forth with their complaints until finally her mother decided it was best for them to continue the conversation another time.

Vaneese was well on her way to setting up her plan to bring her parents story to a fairy tale ending. Next she approached her father with complaints of not having enough allowance to do the things others teens do. She told her father she wanted a car of her own by next year and she should have the sole decision on which college to go to after high school graduation. Her father wasn't use to this assertive side of Vaneese and walked away feeling confused that Vaneese seemed discontent with her lifestyle.

That night her parents talked to each other about their conversations with Vaneese; both expressing their surprise of how unappreciative she seemed to be. This took the focus off of the problems between the two of them for a couple of weeks allowing them to have civil conversations about how to handle Vaneese.

One morning as they gathered at the breakfast table, her father told her they had been discussing the complaints. First he gave her a speech on how less he and her mother had as a child, how hard he worked to provide a better life for his family and how ungrateful teens were today. After the father finished his introduction, her mother told Vaneese how she understood the changes young females go through in their teens. She also told Vaneese that parents have greater responsibilities than to fulfill every wish of their children which included the responsibility first to each other. She explained before meeting Vaneese's father she lived in poverty, lacked education and had no direction in life. She gave him all the credit for helping her focus on pursuing the things that make her life much more meaningful today.

Vaneese waited patiently for this opportunity to bring up the arguments she heard between them. She decided to tell them how it all sounded to her. She told her father, she looked at him as a hero who came to save her mother from being swallowed up by her circumstances. This made the father smile and feel admired by his daughter. She told her mother she believed something about her made her father take notice long enough to invest in helping her get her life together. As an appreciation for what her father did, she felt her mother spent a lot of time trying to make the perfect home for him. Her mother looked at him blushing like a girl who had just met the love of her life.

Vaneese began to tell them both how they seemed to be missing the very thing which brought them to where they are today. She explained how they both focused on each other's need which brought them to the place of achieving their desires. She finished by saying she concluded when needs are overlooked the desires lose their value.

As her parents stood their speechless looking as if a light bulb went off in their heads, Vaneese saw the beginning of the "happily ever after" motto she believed in. She explained to them her contentment for her lifestyle but how she desperately wanted them to see how each other felt when they heard complaints from one another. She also wanted them to see they had both let down each other by being selfishly focused on their own desires which led them to deprive each other of their needs.

Vaneese's mother agreed some of the needs she listed were not needs at all but a way to try and bring the hero back out in him. Her father agreed that his list too was more of a way to show her mother he needed to continue rescuing her. Both parents agreed to each other to put each others needs before their own personal desires. Vaneese walked away feeling she had authored her very own fairy tale with a "happily ever after" ending.

II. THE EXCELLENCE OF ARROGANCE

- The Index Finger

EXCELLENCE:

Possessing valuable qualities in an eminent degree that brings honor and respect

ARROGANCE:

An attitude of superiority presented in an overbearing manner

THIS IS THE ONLY DEFINITION
I DIDN'T ADJUST!

In other words, this definition stands
alone "it is what it is".

However sometimes it's necessary to present excellence in what appears to be an arrogant manner. I coined <u>The Excellence Of Arrogance</u> from this thought:

The attitude of superiority can be important at certain times. When transitioning from one level to a higher level, the people closest to you have a hard time making the mental shift to give you the proper respect for your elevated status. Whether you go from peer to supervisor on a job, preacher to pastor, senator to president - there will be a time frame in which you will have to assert yourself in order to help those closest to you show you the proper respect in that elevation. During these times it's necessary to appear overbearing or ACT superior to expedite the respect in the transition. Politicians are in my opinion the best examples of making transitions because they have a small window of time to work with.

The attitudes we have don't necessarily speak truth to who we are. We can have a position of authority among our peers but it doesn't mean we are superior to them physically or mentally.

In history there have been Kings who've had the best possible tutors to prepare them for their Excellency. Yet, they failed to present qualities in an eminent degree that would bring them merited honor and respect. Possibly when one already knows they will succeed, they have very little motivation to take the preparation serious.

<u>The Excellence Of Arrogance</u> simply means we actually possess valuable qualities that brings honor and respect so therefore we have a responsibility to demand the treatment of superiority.

The reason there is a lack of excellence is because we have been drawn to chasing fads - whatever gains immediate attention or promises of wealth. We have chased many "get rich quick schemes" (Buy Homes With Little Or No Money Down, Internet Stores, and Pyramid Schemes). How many people do you know who have tried these fads are wealthy and happy? I personally don't know any. The greatest excellence comes from those talents and skills that are already noticeable before training. Specialties that come natural to you should be your focus of excellence. Excellence in an area outside of your natural abilities is harder than just building on what you have. If you love to cook, find out more about cooking. There's always something more to ad to what you know. Practice new techniques, try foods outside of your normal recipes and then refine those recipes with your own favorite spices or technique. This can be applied to every talent whether musically inclined, natural artist, great writers, etc. Whatever it is, saturate yourself in all the information, experience or teaching you can on it and then add your own flare to it. Become excellent at being yourself and you will become a person in demand! You will have opportunities to meet people you would have never otherwise met, go places you would have never dared to go and find out things about yourself you may have never known.

Once you develop yourself in your area, you create a new standard in your industry. People will labor to get close to the standard you created. This is one way millionaires are born; wise people have learned to market their excellence.

You can't afford to let a busy schedule, fatigue, or boredom cause you to give "second best". You must have passion for a thing in order to be excellent this is why it's best to concentrate on pursuing your natural talents and abilities. The labor will be demanding to obtain a standard of excellence but once you have achieved that level then its smooth sailing. Once you gain your reputation for excellence word of mouth will keep you in demand. Excellence will entail several grueling years of hard work invested that others may never understand. When others ask why you are working so hard while no one is yet noticing, just reply "my future has noticed". Just remember to keep the "Need/Desire" in its proper perspective. Do it for the love of what you're already good at and not so much for the possible future monetary gain.

THE REWARDS FOR EXCELLENCE ARE GUARANTEED. Whether Emotionally Or Monetarily THE REWARDS FOR EXCELLENCE ARE GUARANTEED!

When you reach your level of excellence, it will be necessary for you to display certain characteristics of arrogance in order to help those closest to you transition to the respect you've earned through your labors.

Arrogance gets a bad rap because of how it was initially defined. To be labeled as arrogant will not win you any social awards however many successful people have an air of arrogance about them. It's in their posture or mannerism but those who understand <u>The Excellence of Arrogance</u> will draw others to seek excellence for their selves. They welcome the opportunity to share who they are with others and it shows. They are not intimidated by the possibility of being duplicated. They understand what it took to get where they are therefore they know there's no way to duplicate who they are without the proper process which takes time that most aren't willing to put into their inner self. Negative arrogant people put most of their time into the external pursuit and they are guarding it with their abrasive attitude. They lack the excellence which brings a confidence that assures the longevity of what they have achieved.

"How much better is it to get wisdom than gold and to get understanding rather to be chosen than silver"

<u>5 Fingers For A Fist Of Power With Peace</u> The Index Finger - is the guide to acceptance of who we are becoming and the importance of making sure others close to us respect

it. In this case there are times you may have to be vocal to guide others in recognizing your elevation. There is arrogance to correcting someone as to how they salute you but would we greet the president or a king by their first or last name rather than their proper salutation? I would hope not because officials usually have someone in their entourage to correct those who do not address them properly. Properly addressing someone you're close to in public is a sign of excellence on your part. It demonstrates your respect level for that person as well as promotes their validity. As the index finger you are to point and guide (direct and apply). When it's your turn to experience elevation, you will know what to expect and how to accept it making for a peaceful but powerful transition.

JUST AVERAGE

Andrew grew up a quiet shy boy with average features, under weight and considered a slow learner. His shyness and average features kept him from being noticed by the girls he wanted to get to know. His physical strength made him least likely to be chosen to participate in athletic events. His lack of ability to grasp the normal subjects in class very fast made him a challenge to the teachers. There was no area in Andrew's life that stood out in a positive way therefore he lacked the attention and respect of his peers.

Andrew was reminded almost daily by those in his life of his inadequacies; taunted and teased about his lack of accomplishments and substandard levels of what they measured as excellence. He began to accept the words of others that meant to him life would never allow him to shine. He resolved to be everyone else's assistant believing this was the closest to being at the top he'd ever get. He took on the odd, the unpopular, dirty and humiliating assignments of those he admired. At home, while his siblings were making their own social strides; Andrew did odd jobs for his parents. He volunteered to help clean up after parties his parents often threw for holidays. Andrew raked leaves and trimmed bushes for his father when he was too tired to do so. Rarely was he shown any appreciation for his volunteered services.

His entire high school years were spent in the shadow of the most popular; the beautiful, young scholars, captains of teams, principal and even the janitor relied on Andrew to do what was labeled meaningless jobs. For the beautiful he carried their books and extra bags so they could maintain their arrogance with those they looked down on. This gave him the inside information on the latest gossip and juiciest news of his schoolmates. The young scholars hired him to research topics they didn't like and to type their homework assignments while they focused on subjects that interested them more. He learned words and ideas that were beyond the normal subjects offered in the school's curriculum.

Andrew maintained the equipment and uniforms of the captains of the basketball and football teams; in exchange, he received free passes to all the games. At times, the most popular students would debate over who Andrew should be most loyal too. Everybody who was somebody wanted the assistance of Andrew. The high demand for Andrews's assistance made him so popular he began to receive additional perks for his services. Andrew received invitations to the best parties, expensive birthday and Christmas gifts, all expense paid vacations with their families and exclusive access to their private clubs. Even his parents started competing for Andrews's attention by offering him privileges such as extended curfews, more access to driving their personal cars and cash loans with no assigned dates for repayment.

Andrew began to see a great benefit for being looked at as an assistant rather than the leader. As he adjusted to the comfortable lifestyle of being in high demand, his confidence in himself increased. His popularity and growing self esteem attracted the friends of the most beautiful and popular girls in high school. As away to win Andrews attention, the girls offered their assistance to him just to be in his presence.

Andrew came to a dilemma in deciding what to do after their high school graduation. It had always been planned by his parents for him to attend a college in another state. His father won the debate with his mother on which college to attend. It had been decided without Andrews input to send him to the college his father attended. Andrew realized he had created an inconspicuous dynasty for himself and wrestled with giving that up. He didn't want to start again from the bottom in a strange city among people who didn't know his value. He knew the only thing to use for leverage in changing the plans of his parents was to convince them they couldn't get along without his assistance. The last few months of his senior year, he increased his assistance with his parents by decreasing his assistance with all others. He knew most of his school mates would be attending local colleges and colleges within their state. His plan was to continue assisting those who remained popular once they started college.

Andrew succeeded in convincing his parents of the value of staying close to home rather than moving away for college. Those he assisted continued to reach out to him for his services. The life he accidentally created for himself continued throughout his college years but the assignments he was given became riskier.

One assignment put Andrew in the company of the mayor of his town. He had been assigned to pass out flyers to the local politicians about the racial and gender profiling the citizens were accusing the local police of. No one wanted this job in fear they would be targeted by crooked and dangerous police who were known to abuse their power and authority. They also were afraid of ruining their reputation among other higher ups, repercussions which could affect their chances for the high profile jobs they had in sight.

The mayor was so impressed with Andrews's boldness; he offered him an internship to assist him. He realized the resourcefulness of Andrew and encouraged him to start his own business. Andrew was so busy with the mayor; he had to relinquish most of his assistance to his old classmates. To their dismay, they panicked at the thought of making decisions, doing research or jobs they had passed on to Andrew in the past. They found they had not developed the necessary skills to climb the ladder of success. As a result they called Andrew begging for his advice on all the subjects they once passed on to him.

Andrew took the advice of the mayor and decided to start his own consulting business. The initial reaction of his family and friends were to discourage him from being independent of them. They did not want to openly acknowledge their need for him because they had grown accustomed to taking all the glory for those things Andrew did behind the scenes.

The challenge he faced was greater than he imagined but realized at some point all leaders faced this same impasse. He feared taking the lead in being a business owner would fail because of his lack of experience in being in the forefront. What he hadn't realized was the assistant positions he once had through out his school years had prepared him for leadership. The mayor began pointing out to him, those rare qualities he had in experience and knowledge.

Andrew accepted the challenge of being the CEO of his own consulting firm although the set up of his company went smoothly the level of respect from those he once served was not shown.

Andrew painfully moved forward in growing his company even though his popularity had hit an all time low in the community of people he knew. They tried to sabotage his company by refusing to use his services, omitting him from their guest lists and the refusal of financial support from his parents. The mayor began to recommend Andrews company to his large network of friends and supporters. The company grew at a record rate without the support of those he once served loyally. Andrew was reaping rewards for maintaining excellence for all those years of serving others. It dawned on him the one thing he was missing in his transition was what every person he served displayed. They carried themselves as if they deserved to be treated a certain way and their arrogant demeanor demanded the respect of others. As painful as it was to be rejected socially by this friends and family, when forced to be in their company he walked among them with a posture of entitlement. His attitude was read loud and clear; he insisted on being recognized as leader and dismissed any contradictory gestures.

When his old acquaintances realized they weren't able to make the strides they once enjoyed with his assistance, they slowly reached out to him for professional help. Not all were willing to acknowledge him but those that did, did so through his lesson of the excellence of arrogance.

III. THE STUBBORN LIFE OF THE STRONG WILLED

- The Middle Finger

STUBBORN:

Unreasonably determined to be resistant by being difficult

It is impossible to have a fulfilling life with stubbornness as a strong personality trait. This trait gives a false sense of power and control but ultimately stubbornness lessens the quality of life one could be living. There is no productive reason to be stubborn which indicates to me stubbornness is caused by fear and pride. Fear of the unknown, change and progress can cause someone to resist exploring other possibilities.

Stubbornness can be caused by past failures, heartbreaks and other tough lessons of life. The memory of those bad outcomes induces a self talk that plays out all the possible reasons why you shouldn't go along with an opportunity. Fear can be crippling and highly destructive. You should weigh options and consequences before acting so that you can plan your strategy carefully. When weighing the options and consequences causes you to abandon your goals, then you are operating in fear. Fear is destructive because it can cause us to turn a death ear to great advice and turn our backs on great opportunities that have the potential to get us to where we desire to go quicker. Eliminating fear comes through trial and error. Learning how to regroup after making a bad decision is a necessary part of maturity. Stubborn people suffer internally while looking strong externally. They are normally hiding a very immature side of themselves.

Pride fuels fear while fear fuels pride, they are a marriage made in misery. They depend on each other to function at their peak. When pride and fear are cooperating, nothing can stop them from accomplishing their goal which is to the render the carrier lifeless. I personally believe they are roots of depression, anxiety, suicide and most destructive behaviors. Pride is deceptive in that it can seem honorable to be proud but when used as a camouflage of fear, it only brings discomfort to the carrier and eventually to those closely associated with them. It's natural to be proud of an accomplishment but when that accomplishments future is threatened, the seed of fear begins to grow. When we have been displaying our pride in an accomplishment, we can feel the need to keep pride on display even in the face of fear. The more fear grows the harder we tend to work at hiding it, this is when the destructive part of pride appears. I call it false pride because the initial proud feeling of the accomplishment that was healthy has now turned into a hypocritical since of pride. The pride of being proud turns into stubbornness because we are trying to preserve the moment we felt the true pride of an accomplishment. The fear of an unraveling accomplishment being exposed continues to fuel pride. This creates a vicious cycle that can go on until a person self destructs entirely. It is imperative to break free from this cycle and it can only be done by honestly exposing the fear to those who have a healthy sense of themselves. Those who have nothing to gain from your circumstance, those who have conquered stubbornness and have pure motives in life are your best source of counsel. You have to find a safe place or person to express your fears.

> *"Pride goes before destruction and a*
> *haughty spirit before a fall"*

STRONG WILLED:

Having a determined will, determined to prevail in the face of difficulty or opposition

Strong willed is based off of proven facts through experience that a certain thing will or will not work for you. Even if it has worked for someone else, we must realize that everything isn't for everyone. Standing firm on a conviction, lesson learned through experience or in principles we choose to govern our lives by will protect us from proven negative outcomes.

There will always be people who give unsolicited advice; it's just a way for some people to feel productive. Most people who give unsolicited advice actually have great things to say. It's not that they aren't giving good advice but it's just not quite the advice that will work for your situation. When people try to force you to take their advice, I suggest you put some distance between yourself and those kinds of people. If you are caught between your own opinion of what you should do in a matter and someone else's, I recommend following your own gut, instinct, conviction or principle. Even if you're wrong, the experience can be valuable to your future. We should never let others rob us of experience, every great person has made great mistakes but they learned from them and stored the knowledge to apply in future situations.

This is how you can develop a strong will: you go forward with an ideal and it works very well for you, you practice working what you've learned until its second nature mainly because you continue to see positive results.

The continued success strengthens your conviction and the conviction becomes a principle. When someone tries to get you to change you're principle, your strong-will shows up through you insisting on doing what has proven affective for you. At these times a power struggle can ensue and it becomes necessary to star in, <u>The Stubborn Life Of The Strong Willed</u>. At times you will have to be unreasonably determined to stand on what your conviction's are.

I have lost acquaintances (people I thought were friends) through these times and I do not resent making my stands. If my friendship with a person is contingent upon me taking their advice, then it's no friendship but rather a dictatorship. Therefore, I am better off without those types of people in my life. My life is simplified, I have a greater peace when I don't have to struggle with others about the decisions I make for my life.

It should be the job of the other(s) to convince you through more than words that their advice is better than your conviction. There have been times I've decided to take someone else's advice against my better judgment. Sometimes it's been because I was unsure of the untested waters, sometimes it's been because I highly respected the other person and other times I was too frustrated with a situation to make a decision on my own. Most times, when I decided against my own instinct or judgment, I was wrong in taking the other persons advice. I don't have an exact percentage but I would guess 90% of the time, I've been disappointed in not following my own gut, instinct or proven method of decision making in certain areas. I don't despise advice and we all can use it, but to learn to trust our own experiences to help us make decisions for ourselves is how we become Independently Liberated.

When we are constantly taking other peoples advice then we aren't ourselves but we are who our advice comes from.

5 Fingers For A Fist Of Power With Peace The Middle Finger - Besides the thumb, I believe the middle finger is very important because of its length and strength. It is like a pillar of the hand because it firmly grips what the hand has grasped. Once you have accepted a concept or principal it takes a strong will to enforce your stance. The strength of the middle finger can be an illustration of saying; even if I stand alone I'm going to stand. *"When who we are is over ridden by what we want then what we want becomes who we are"*. If you want to be taken serious, you have to have certain standards that you stand on in the face of all adversity. This is another way to gain respect and with respect there is peace and power.

BRED TO BELIEVE IN BERTHA

Ms Bertha Sims was the talk of the town but not because she was liked rather because she was a "Ms know it all".

Bertha grew up in a household of well educated wealthy grandparents. Her parents died in a car accident when she was 2; so her grandparents raised her as their own. Bertha's grandparents were too elderly to raise her without assistance so they hired the best tutors money could acquire. At age 3 she was learning an additional language, piano and dance; by age 5 she was on her third language speaking fluently in English, Spanish and French. Her governess better known as a nanny, who knew 7 languages was picked based on her impressive resume. It boasted of her extensive knowledge of world affairs, teaching abilities, the many countries she had traveled, royal connections and excellent references for raising children to exemplify superior qualities.

When there were any gaps between her assignments with her governess, Bertha was instructed to spend time in the extensive library of her grandparents'. The expectation from her grandparents was for her to read one book per week with the ability to fully comprehend its content.

Bertha only knew pressure, performance and the expectation to commit to learning how to expound on every subject imaginable.

There was very little time for Bertha to make friends and play childhood games. She was sheltered to the extent that she only knew how to have conversations with the highly educated or experienced adults. Her governess was employed until Bertha turned 12 at which time she was sent to the best boarding school in Paris. As a part of her education, she spent a year at a convent, two years aiding the hungry in various third world countries and three years assisting medical teams in war zones. Those experiences left her cold and hardened because emotions were discouraged in order to keep the interns focused on their tasks.

Bertha's college experience was the best all girls college on the East Coast of the United States. Even among those well rounded highly educated young ladies, Bertha excelled above them all. She surpassed them in experience and knowledge and understanding of how the issues of the entire world played an important part in how our own government conducts its foreign affairs.

The other students were drawn to her and she in return told those stories of her life in war zones, the convent and third world countries. Every day someone wanted to know more about her unorthodox upbringing. She had a need to be heard and to share what seemed like novels of information in her head. The dialog was always one-sided because the others were too intrigued with Bertha to interrupt one of her stories with inquiries.

When the others attempted to have a conversation with Bertha on world subjects, they realized there was no room for error. Bertha often reminded them of her superior education and training as well as the number of books she had read on every subject imaginable. At times the other girls would make suggestions to Bertha about her appearance and the lack of experience socializing with the opposite sex. Her grandparents neglected to teach her how to dress appropriate for her age and social skills with the male species. Bertha wore very conservative clothes and hairstyles which made her look 10 years older than her age. She refused to go with the other young ladies to parties that weren't high profile. They used her appearance as a weapon and incompetent social skills against her when she seemed to be too high on her horse; it was the only way they felt they could even the playing field. Her lack of knowledge in fashion and social adjustment to those her age began to haunt her.

She never had time to watch television, go to movies or out on dates because she was constantly in training and learning political subjects. It was clear now there were important areas in her life she had not been properly prepared for. Any suggestion given her was met with a rebuttal that normally could not be challenged. She easily dominated her opponents with her inexhaustible vocabulary. Her experience and exposure to real life experiences; gave her a good idea of what worked and what didn't work.

As a preventive method, Bertha picked intellectual fights with anyone who threatened to expose her weaknesses. She stayed quiet until she sized up her opponent then made mockery of their weakness before they had an opportunity to expose hers. Her purpose was to put fear into anyone who seemed bold enough to make suggestions to her. Bertha's arguments made her the least liked person in college. Her reputation for being stubborn drove away the other young ladies in her dorm, classes and sorority. They use to enjoy the stories of her adventures and were impressed with her adapting to so many cultures while abroad. Her stubborn abrasive ways had now over shadowed all the good characteristics once admired by her college mates.

The loneliness of alienation made Bertha depressed and suicidal. Bertha contemplated killing herself but her religious beliefs weighed on her conscious. She was sad none of the girls were inviting her to go home with them during school breaks. Her grandparents had died the year she entered college; her dorm mates use to draw straws to decide who would get the right to take Bertha home with them. Since Bertha had pushed everyone away with her stubbornness; she had nowhere to go any more. No grandparents or distant relatives and now no friends who could tolerate her abrasiveness.

Bertha decided to do what she was taught to do; pick up a book on any subject she wanted to master. For months she read and studied books on making friends, relationships with men and fashion.

She reached out to her dorm mates with individual written apologies and an invitation to a party she planned to reunite with them. She had learned in her studies of friendships and relationships to value others knowledge. She told them of the lessons learned from their absence. They let her know they didn't think it necessary to change those things she knew worked. Everyone agreed she should remain strong in her convictions but without crushing the feelings of her friends.

She began to try suggestions on clothes and dating from the others; some things worked for her while others didn't. She had forgotten how much fun it was learning something new. She had been under the impression she could only learn from those with more education and experience than herself.

The deflation of her ego helped her understand the value of stubbornness, the times it is most valuable and the times when it's least valued. Bertha was surprised she could learn from those she knew didn't have the same advantages her grandparents exposed her to. She now understood the balance of sticking with what was proven to work but staying open to accepting knowledge from those she wanted relationships with. In the end, her stubborn experiences helped her identify the benefits of a strong will.

IV. THE INDEPENDENTLY LIBERATED

- The Ring Finger

INDEPENDENT:

Existence not contingent on anything or anyone else's control

Given the definition created from my mixture of information....no one is really independent. We all rely on something and or someone to exist. The experience's that mold us into productive beings have come through people, places and things. Those people, places and things are not the root of our existence therefore they should not control who we are. What defines our independence is the choice to use those experiences as building blocks to our personal goals.

We lose our sense of independence when we set aside our personal goals because of pressures that come from people we want in our lives, places that can't accommodate our way of thinking and things (economics and politics) that seem to be unmovable road blocks. We cause others to lose their independence by pressuring them to conform to our personal goals. Our motives must not be selfish so we don't become a hindrance to ourselves and to others who are trying to accomplish their personal goals. When our assistance is no longer needed, we have to learn how to gracefully move aside without bringing chaos to that person's transition. We must learn how to help others accept when their assistance is no longer needed by assuring them that their assistance was appreciated and valued.

There's always turbulence in maintaining independence but it levels out once your circle of support understands your independence is not a detachment but rather a work of interdependence. The people who accept your independence will become pillars in your progress rather than weights that must be cut off. Interdependence is a healthy ingredient in sound relationships because there's a balance of assistance to each other. When there's no fear of each other's independence, progress can be made at a greater pace for all involved. You cannot experience interdependence without at least two independent people.

The greater the circle of cooperative independent people in your life, the more progress will be for all involved.

We have to allow each other to work out as many of the problems related to our goals as possible on our own. We have to learn to ask for help when we have exhausted all our resources to help ourselves. It doesn't take away our independence to need help unless we give it away by conforming to another mindset in order to get the immediate relief from our existing obstacle. There is a task in finding people to connect with on the level that infuses interdependence.

You may start out with many who can only go so far with you but hopefully you will find another independent person to link with for the next level of your progression. You will know when you've found a person to connect with because their energy and enthusiasm will motivate you to ignite or reignite your desire. You will also know when it's time to disconnect because they will start to have the opposite affect on you....draining you by means of neediness, over protectiveness and lack of encouragement to you. Disconnect doesn't mean discard the friendship or acquaintance it just means they can't be a part of the process of your greater goal. You can choose to let them enjoy the benefits of your gain without being a part of the full process. Sometimes that's exactly how marriages work, your spouse may not be the wind beneath your wings but your love for them allows you to share the benefits of your successes.

LIBERATED:

Freed from or opposed to traditional social and sexual attitudes or roles

Even though I believe there are certain steps to keeping one's essence at the forefront of a productive life - I believe it's necessary to be careful not to take what we know and teach it in a way that drives others to believe cloning themselves after someone else will bring them the fulfillment they seek. In all the understanding we derive from life's experiences, every person's experiences should produce a personal gain. My experience's keep me Independently Liberated. Most people enjoy my company; they're interested in what's going on in my life. If they've spent any significant amount of time with me, they know I am strong-willed but I have an open invitation to the independents.

Being free from what others think about your decisions is necessary for a life that is fulfilling internally. A free thinker can appear to be obstinate because they break away from tradition, attitudes and roles put in place by others. When you think of certain holidays, there are traditions that most of our society expects us to participate in. When you free yourself to break from that norm you have become liberated. It doesn't mean you won't celebrate that holiday it just means you won't follow some or all of the associated traditions. There are times when our liberation frees others to test their own liberties they may have otherwise never tried had they not seen someone close to them practice liberation. Liberation is not about breaking moral codes, being defiant or aggravating the masses but more about freedom to choose when and when not to conform to traditions, attitudes and roles. Great events of the world happened with the <u>Independently Liberated</u> thinker at the helm. It's hard for me to imagine liberation without independence mainly because the very act of being liberated can cause a lot of lonely times. Before people understand what you're trying to accomplish, your actions may appear to be too radical for them to trust that you know where you're going. When you step outside of the norm, you're the guinea pig. You will be watched for the results, if you succumb to the pressures of tradition after making a bold stance against it, then you lose credibility with the observers. Your success is what gives power to others so it's important to have a reason for your actions and not act for the sake of doing something different. *"When who we are is over ridden by what we want then what we want becomes who we are"*.

5 Fingers For A Fist Of Power With Peace The Ring Finger - This is the finger that solidifies the interdependence of the relationship of all the components it takes to make a fist. It is close in rank with the middle finger but plays a support role without dominating the others. The power of support to our independence gives us the opportunity to play a role in liberating others. We are not cloning ourselves but we are combining independent efforts with other independents to expedite the goals of each other. The power of the hand is when all fingers (which have independent functions) form an interdependence (called the fist) to make an impact that benefits all…separately and corporately.

REBELS RULE

This story is about a young lady named Katy who was raised by one parent. Katherine left Bryan when Katy was 8 because of irreconcilable differences. Katherine knew she couldn't raise the child on her own and agreed to let Bryan raised her without any interference. Bryan was convinced Katherine would someday return; expecting financial hardship to drive her back to him.

He drove Katherine away with strict house rules and narrow minded ideas about marriage. His childhood rearing was from his father, a devout Catholic who himself was schooled by the hard discipline practices of elderly nuns. He was taught by his father there could be only one authority figure per household. His mother seemed to understand the rules; there weren't any conflict between his parents that he knew of.

Katherine was not allowed to discipline their daughter; only attend to her personal care such as feeding, clothing and bathing. She was to keep Katy out of trouble but not allowed to correct any bad behavior; to report the actions to him for discipline decisions. Katherine rarely reported anything to Bryan out of rebellion to his strictness; protecting Katy from what she considered close to child abuse.

She had no say over what to buy, how to decorate the home or anything that meant change. She was not allowed to change her hair, wear make-up or buy store bought clothes. Bryan was very set in his ways and thought changing one thing meant everything associated would be affected by the change. One day Katherine changed the living room furniture around, when Bryan returned home he was furious to see the change. He scolded her for taking an initiative calling it a lack of respect for his role as the head of the household. He accused her of trying to slowly manipulate him into changing everything about their life.

Once Katy was secure with school and adapting well to a more liberal environment; Katherine felt comfortable making her break from Bryan and moved six hundred miles away to Indiana. Katherine had a degree in Business Administration but never was allowed to work outside the home once she married Bryan. She secretly applied for jobs through agencies when Bryan went to work. Her first and only response was for a newly developed business in Indiana.

Katy was left to live alone under the strict rules of her father. The main rule for Katy was to always ask her father when a choice was offered. Katy never raised her hand in school when asked for suggestions and wouldn't answer any questions that required choices she had never been given instruction on. Since she was a well behaved student, the teachers didn't approach their concerns to Bryan; however whispers of him being odd and raising a daughter alone went on between the facultures.

Katherine was allowed to call Katy once a month but only if she spent her first fifteen minutes listening to Bryan's lecture on why she was wrong for leaving. After three years of not convincing her to return, Bryan decided it was best for her to only write Katy.

Katherine knew her only choices were to return or comply; the thought of returning made her have severe headaches. Her plan was to keep enough contact with Katy so when she was of age, she would feel free to move to Indiana.

For five years she wrote to Katy every month, sending birthday cards and gifts she knew Bryan would accept.

When Katy turned sixteen, she started asking to visit her mother in Indiana; making a case for herself by expressing how obedient she had always been for him. Bryan dismissed the idea without hesitation stating things had to stay the same. Katy challenged him by reminding him of the changes he made from phone calls to letters only. Bryan put her on a month restriction for disrespecting his authority.

That month, Katherine sent her normal package of a gift and letter to Katy only to receive it back marked, 'Return To Sender'. Katherine called Bryan and was not pleased with his explanation; demanding to talk to Katy. Bryan told her never to call or write again because Katy didn't want to go through not having a mother in the home. She was never to see or hear from Katy again.

Katherine knew this was not the words of her daughter and in her fury she told Bryan things she had once concealed. "Your mother told me in confidence; she hated your father but only stayed because she was afraid of living without the security of being provided with shelter and food. She knew he was not going to ever change and hoped it wouldn't affect her children. She knew I was unhappy with you because you were most like your father of all her children. Before she died she told me I should leave while I had a chance and take Katy with me. My only regret is that I did one part without doing the other. You won't be able to keep her away from me forever". Katherine hung up and never tried to call again but decided to send Katy letters through friends and neighbors who supported her leaving Bryan.

Bryans friends could see how the strict practices towards Katy was crippling her chances for being independent some day. The wives of his buddies convinced their husbands to intervene by introducing him to available women his age; offering to let their wives baby-sit Katy for free to give him a break. Still holding on to the hope Katherine would return, Bryan refused to entertain the thought of dating or remarrying.

Katy was bitter against her father for trying to totally shut down her relationship with her mother. Katy was growing bitter with her mother for leaving her alone with her father who was only capable of making the women he loved hate him.

She had received a letter from her mother sent to their neighbor; it explained in detail why she left without her. Katy decided to cut off communication with her mother and handle her father alone.

Katy purposely did poorly in school, challenged her father's rules by staying out with friends until dark, changing her hair and wearing make-up. She knew her father would not put her out because she was the only tool he could use to possible get her mother back; plus without her, he would be totally alone in their big lifeless house.

No matter how severely Bryan punished Katy; she continued to rebel by smoking and drinking, calling boys and wearing revealing clothes.

The more Katy rebelled the better she felt; her taste of liberty was addicting and growing. She was less bitter with her mother because she understood independence was an extreme opposite of the life with her father. As soon as Katy turned 18 she moved to Indiana with her mother but instead of it being a free for all; her mother had rules. They were not nearly as strict as her fathers but in Katy's mind it contradicted the reasons her mother left.

Katy's mother explained to her the importance of being independent and making decisions of her own. She emphasized the importance of having liberty without doing something that could jeopardize her independence. Katy spent the next few years learning from her mother how to be independently liberated.

V. THE HUMBLENESS OF PASSIVITY

- The Pinky Finger

HUMBLE:

Willingly submissive to equal counterparts to promote the significance of others

PASSIVE:

Lacking the will to be active, open or direct therefore yielding to dominant influences.

HUMBLE THOUGHT! Being able to walk in ones accomplishments with confidence without demanding the accolades through self publication.

PASSIVE THOUGHT! Unable to express confidence in the presence of superior or dominant personalities.

I have seen many people consider their selves humble when actually they are acting passive. When the presence of a certain person pushes you into a shell or you think you have to dummy down around them; that's passiveness not humility. I have seen children be energetic and happy around one parent but when the other (more dominant) parent arrives they sink into a mousy demeanor. I have watched coworker's fellowship until the supervisor walks in the room then their tone with each other becomes unsure. I have seen passive dogs (usually they have been abused) and I have seen humble dogs (they are secure in their place in a family).

You cannot express who you really are for any length of time when you are completely passive. It is difficult to continue to switch from one state of mind to another; therefore it's safer to display the passive characteristics at all times. Passivity robs you of experiences that will endorse <u>The Stubborn Life of The Strong-Willed</u>. You will never know what works for you and you will never establish a standard by being completely passive. You will be continually in the shadow of those YOU choose to be the dominant forces in your life.

Passive people can be great at being chameleons; they adapt themselves to their surroundings to keep from bringing aggressive attention to themselves. When put in a situation where there are more than one dominating personalities, they almost blend in with the wall paper-saying or doing very little to avoid the possibility of being put in a place to choose which dominating personality to conform to. Some passive people become very popular with dominating personalities because there isn't any competing involved. Passive people disturb those who think no one should be so adaptable to everyone.

I conclude the shame of passivity has caused many to re-label their selves as humble. Passiveness is a result of a broken will which has to be repaired by a determination to living a life that teaches you to live. I personally dealt with passivity for a very long time; it was a prison within me. I felt like there were bars on my mind and concrete walls around my physical being. Passive people are in a complete prison, mentally and physically.

Passivity is mainly enforced by harsh criticism. When a passive person tries to crawl out of their shell, the dominant beneficiary lashes them with harsh criticism over the simplest error. Harsh criticism can act as a whip and chain bringing embarrassing pain to the already passive person. Another tool against the passive is deprivation which I won't get into in this book. Just be aware that if someone says they care for you but they deprive you of things they have in their power to give to you, it's possible there's an impure motive behind that act.

When you're already broken it's hard to imagine being whole. It's easier to avoid the pain of harsh criticism than to take a stand. They are the ones who need to see liberation in action which triggers some hope. Passive people are lured into secluding themselves from the aggressive and assertive world. They are convinced that they will not suffer any additional brokenness if they hide as much as possible. When they are confronted with people, they tend to be overly accommodating and avoid any possible negative responses towards them. It is a torture that can't be described to its fullest extent, to experience it is the only real way to sympathize with those captured in that state.

Passivity in a healthy person - in an independent person is not out of fear but out of confidence. The whole idea of distinguishing between the two is to bring awareness to the broken passive person that what they are experiencing is mental abuse - whether it comes from a parent, spouse, boss or friend. Those who abuse with criticism are usually afraid your independence will cause you to leave them behind. If they are too stubborn to change from that abusive behavior then fear is their fuel and pride is its coconspirator.

The accomplished independent person can humbly celebrate the small steps of others trying to find their way. They understand humbleness doesn't take away from the essence of who they are. Passive people can find hope in a true humble person; most humble people have experienced passivity and brokenness of some kind. The new and improved person who has gained their independence and excellence can guide the broken spirit of others to new.

Humbleness Of Passivity is a way of honoring yourself and others. Yourself in that your confidence allows you to make room for someone else's excellence. Some passivity has its place especially when it comes to adapting to new surroundings. Initially passivity is a great way to learn from the outside looking in but there's a limit to what is learned through observation. When the peak of learning something is reached, humbleness can take you to the next peak.

5 Fingers For A Fist Of Power With Peace The Pinky Finger - Seems to be the least credible finger of the fist. We may not feel there is much use to this finger however it still brings honor to the hand. It is reverenced as the completeness of the hand because it locks in what may have tried to escape through the gap left in the ring finger. It waits for the opportunity to assist in the clinching of the fist and doesn't demand any attention for its contribution. When you consider your value of which you are, there is no need to be threatened by those who are excellent in their field. Your willingness to allow someone else to shine makes you valuable without the fan fare. When it's your turn to be recognized, people will be more amazed by your competence because of your humble stance. This may seem a little contrary to the <u>Excellence of Arrogance</u> but it isn't because the demand for respect is not something you have to do continual but the <u>Humbleness of Passivity</u> will be useful in every arena.

CHUMPED BY CHARM

It took many years of insults and criticism for Brent to figure out how to change how people perceived him. His inability to speak up for himself made him a moving target for every bully on the block. Brent's mother was determined not to spoil her only son, who was already showing signs of entitlement by charming his grandparents into giving him the best of everything.

Brent entertained his grandparents with stunts, silly faces and off the wall comments. He was great at making others laugh especially the elderly grownups. When they went to the bank, Brent would entertain and charm the tellers into giving him suckers. When they went to McDonalds he would smile and make funny faces at the cashier; in exchange he received free fries and toys. At day care, he charmed the care workers by helping, following the rules and playing nicely with the other children. Everywhere he went, he found a way to charm the adults. It was a little more challenging to charm other children, many of them were jealous of his ability to win over the adults.

Brent's mother demanded his father put a stop to this trend being set by the grandparents. His father had no back bone when it came to his own parents so he decided to work on the behavior of Brent. When they saw Brent charming his grandparents, he was severely punished and scolded once the grandparents left. They noticed Brent was losing his charming ways and concluded someone was interfering. They questioned Brent assuring him they would keep what he told them a secret. Brent was relieved to let them know he had not changed but was trying to avoid the punishments of his father. Brent's grandparents made a promise to him to continue giving him the things he liked without putting him at risk in front of his father. Brent thought his grandparents had to be the smartest people in the world to be able to keep everyone happy.

Now that his grandparents were back in hand, he had to figure out a way to get back on the good side of his playmates. Most of them looked at adults as the enemy of all children; no adult was to be trusted. They treated him like a traitor until he shifted his loyalties in front of them. He pretended not to like the adults when other children were around; pouring on the charm when he was alone with the adults made up for his poor behavior displayed around the other children.

Brent mastered charming both the adults and pretending to have an allegiance with the other children; learning from his grandparents to adjust. Brent's grandparents knew only to spoil him when he was at their house otherwise they played along with what worked to keep Brent safe from being punished.

Once Brent entered grade school, it became difficult to shift back and forth between the adults and his friends. It was a rare moment when there wasn't both an adult and one of his friends around at the same time. Fearing being exposed as two faced, he became inverted; Brent turned his charm completely off, no more joking and entertaining anyone. To his friends, he was no longer fun to be around. When they tried including him in their mischief against the teachers, he just sat their silent. He was tortured by his fears making every moment at school miserable. The only relief he felt was when visiting his grandparents, they continued their agreement. Brent pretended to be sick most of the school year because the pressure was too much for him to handle. He had been forced into passivity; the power of his charm had made most people in his life uncomfortable one way or the other.

Brent learned to be fun and funny without an ulterior motive; to like people for who they were instead of what he could get from them. With his change, he saw a change in everyone he cared for; both adults and friends started to respect him. He no longer had to be passive to please people; the humility he showed by changing had more power than passivity.

VI. 5 FINGERS FOR A FIST OF POWER WITH PEACE

–A Hand Makes A Fist

Imagine life without a thumb, you can accomplish many things but the stress and strain to hold onto something without it can be frustrating. The thumb simplifies our lives and this is what identifying needs verses desires should do. There is a power and peace in having your needs met because you have established structure by putting desires in their proper place.

The Index Finger is the guide to acceptance of who we are becoming and the importance of making sure others close to us respect it. In this case there are times you may have to be vocal to guide others in recognizing your elevation. There is arrogance to correcting someone as to how they salute you but would we greet the president or a king by their first or last name rather than their proper salutation? I would hope not because officials usually have someone in their entourage to correct those who do not address them properly. Properly addressing someone you're close to in public is a sign of excellence on your part. It demonstrates your respect level for that person as well as promotes their validity. As the index finger you are to point and guide (direct and apply). When it's your turn to experience elevation, you will know what to expect and how to accept it making for a peaceful but powerful transition.

Besides the thumb, I believe the middle finger is very important because of its length and strength. It is like a pillar of the hand because it firmly grips what the hand has grasped. Once you have accepted a concept or principal it takes a strong will to enforce your stance. The strength of the middle finger can be an illustration of saying; even if I stand alone I'm going to stand. *"When who we are is over ridden by what we want then what we want becomes who we are"*. If you want to be taken serious, you have to have certain standards that you stand on in the face of all adversity. This is another way to gain respect and with respect there is peace and power.

The ring finger solidifies the interdependence of the relationship of all the components it takes to make a fist. It is close in rank with the middle finger but plays a support role without dominating the others. The power of support to our independence gives us the opportunity to play a role in liberating others. We are not cloning ourselves but we are combining independent efforts with other independents to expedite the goals of each other. The power of the hand is when all fingers (which have independent functions) form an interdependence (called the fist) to make an impact that benefits all…separately and corporately.

We may not feel there is much use for the pinky finger however it still brings honor to the hand. It is reverenced as the completeness of the hand because it locks in what may have tried to escape through the gap left in the ring finger. It waits for the opportunity to assist in the clinching of the fist and doesn't demand any attention for its contribution. When you consider your value of which you are, there is no need to be threatened by those who are excellent in their field. Your willingness to allow someone else to shine makes you valuable without the fan fare. When it's your turn to be recognized, people will be more amazed by your competence because of your humble stance. This may seem a little contrary to the Excellence of Arrogance but it isn't because the demand for respect is not something you have to do continual but the Humbleness of Passivity will be useful in every arena.

STRANGE POWER

8 A.M on a Friday morning, five college students who never knew each other before the first day living in a

dorm, met with great expectation of having the time of their lives as Freshmen in college. This dorm was coed and these particular cohabiters were a ratio of three young ladies and two young men. JeLisha grew up in Compton, CA under the average conditions for an African American girl in the tough streets of a neighborhood like hers. She had not settled on a major but signed up for Psychology because it sounded interesting. Cameron, a middle class young Caucasian grew up in Los Angeles, CA where he was introduced to famed musicians because his father was a great drummer. Cameron's desire was to be an agent and manager in the music industry. Romella's mother was Hispanic and her father Caucasian, they moved from Texas when she was ten years old to San Bernardino, CA. Romella didn't want to be at college but was forced there by her father. DeAndre was the son of a well known African American lawyer in Hollywood whose ambition was to take over his fathers' law firm. Cassy who also grew up in Hollywood was the daughter of an Asian hairdresser who had formerly been a high paid call girl. She didn't know who her father was; he was possibly one of the many clients her mother had. Cassy's decided to major in Business Management and eventually set up a string of hair salons.

They drew straws for bedrooms then made out a calendar for duties in cleaning, private time in the common room and rules for having company over. Things were going smoothly, they helped each other unpack and set up their bedrooms. While sharing a little about themselves, they found several common interests between the five of them. It was obvious they could be a really powerful group because of their strengths which came from their individual challenges of growing up. JeLisha's greatest challenge was graduating high school without becoming a teen mother; Cameron was challenged with resisting the use of drugs and alcohol he was exposed to by his fathers' musician friends; Romella's challenge was to be accepted as a legal citizen in the United States; DeAndre's challenge was being displaced as a young black man - not being accepted by many blacks because of where he lived and not being accepted by whites because he was black; Cassy acknowledged she had an identity crisis because she never knew her father and because of her mother's reputation of being a prostitute. They made a pack to be a team and look out for each other like a family.

They all agreed to go club hopping their first night together as a way to continue bonding and to make other friends. The girls seemed to be drawn to JeLisha because she had great taste in clothes. She helped the girls get ready for the club with their outfits while Cassy gave tips on hairstyles do's and don'ts she had learned from her mother. The guys immediately complimented the girls as they joined them in the common room of the dorm. The girls snickered teasing that DeAndre was dressed like he was going to church rather than a club and convinced him to lose the tie and suit jacket. Cameron won the ooo's and ahhh's of the girls with his hip look that stated he was versatile.

Everyone agreed with DeAndre's suggestion to established team rules for going out. The rules were not to leave each other alone and not to leave the club without everyone being accounted for; no one would go home before everyone agreed or with someone not from their group and no one was going to invite anyone to their dorm for after hour partying. As they entered the first club, Romella suggested they all get on the dance floor together as a group to start off mingling. JeLisha disagreed saying dancing with a group and especially with other girls would make them look gay. Cassy was upset that JeLisha obviously had a problem with someone else's opinion as well as someone else's sexuality. The guys were in total agreement with Romella's idea and headed to the dance floor, Romella and Cassy followed leaving JeLisha by herself at the table.

After fifteen minutes of dancing, the others returned back to the table to find JeLisha pouting and complaining that she was left alone. Even though they all apologized, JeLisha refused to accept accusing them all of being racist and arrogant. DeAndre began to defend himself with the fact that he too was African American and didn't see any signs of racism within the group especially since all but Cameron were from minority groups. Cameron defended the fact that as a musician's son he was exposed to every nationality of musician there was. The rest of the night they followed the rule of not leaving anyone alone. DeAndre took on the responsibility of keeping everyone informed of the rules since he initiated them. After an hour at the first club, they went to a second club where a live band was playing. Cassy spotted three different guys she intended on getting their numbers before they left; Romella promised to help her with her quest. Secretly, Romella was interested in one of the three guys Cassy had her eye on. Cameron was intrigued by the female drummer who played like a pro and as soon as the band broke for a break, Cameron made his move to introduce himself to the drummer. They connected immediately and she pushed to see him after the club let out but he explained the rules set up by the group. She decided she wouldn't come to their dorm but that there wasn't anything in the rules saying once the group returned to the dorm he couldn't go out. Cameron agreed to meet her after the group returned to the dorm; they exchanged numbers and flirted with glances as often as they could. Cameron began to casually suggest to the group not stay out too late on their first outing but everyone ignored him.

DeAndre talked JeLisha into dancing with him as an attempt to calm her down; she anxiously followed him to the dance floor. As they danced JeLisha began to complain about each of the others; accusing Cassy of being sluttish and possibly bisexual; Romella of being a gold digger and party girl; and Cameron had to be into drugs and possibly of the Arian Nation. DeAndre shook his head wanting to know what she really thought of him, explaining to her sometimes growing up in bad neighborhoods makes people suspicious of everyone. He made her promise to give each person a chance to prove themselves stating it will take a few months to truly know each other's personality. JeLisha had developed a crush on DeAndre; not only was he handsome and well dressed but he was the coolest, nicest upper class African American man she had ever met.

Actually, he was the only middle class man of her nationality she had ever met. Her perception of people like him was they would never take the time to get to know her because of the neighborhood she came from. They danced a few dances before Romella insisted DeAndre dance with her, JeLisha walked away rolling her eyes at Romella in jealousy.

Romella explained to DeAndre she wanted to dance with him to get close to the guy she was eyeing and he agreed to help her get close enough to talk to him. DeAndre had not expressed any interest in any of the roommates or any girls from either club, his focus was on becoming a great lawyer. He had already discussed with his father the downfalls of getting emotionally involved while at college working on a career major. DeAndre respected his father highly and would do nothing to disappoint him. As they danced closer, Romella asked the guy to dance with her so they exchanged dance partners. DeAndre danced off with the girl winking at Romella and Romella winked back as she mouthed a thank you. Romella managed to get the number of Drew, the guy Cassy liked that she liked too but decided not to give the number to Cassy. She had already helped Cassy get the number of the first two guys of interest and felt it was more than enough for one girl on one night.

Cameron made a final attempt to get the group to go home, JeLisha sided with him because of her anger with Romella for cutting in on her and DeAndre; DeAndre sided because he didn't want to get into any situations with the girls that were making eyes at him; Romella sided because she didn't want Cassy to get Drew's number; Cassy decided since she was out numbered not to make waves.

No one said much to each other on the walk home but the tension was obvious. In one evening the bond from earlier had been broken. Cameron called his new drummer friend as soon as they reached the dorm while Romella went to the bathroom to secretly call Drew. The others enquired of Romella and Cameron about their plans to go back out that night. Cameron explained he was not breaking any rules by going back out, the agreement was to stay together while out and come home together. No one could dispute him, so Romella took the opportunity to make plans to see Drew later. JeLisha could no longer hold in her anger and decided to recap the entire night accusing everyone of betraying her. Romella defended herself for cutting in on JeLisha and DeAndre's dance explaining she was getting a phone number from Drew. Cassy argued with Romella calling her a backstabber for getting Drew's number while Romella defended why she didn't give up Drew's number. DeAndre explained to JeLisha he was only dancing with her to calm her down not to come onto her and he was not trying to get involved with anyone while he studied. After everything was out in the open, Romella left to meet Drew while Cameron left to meet his drummer friend and the others went to their separate rooms confused and angry.

The next day no one talked to each other until Cameron broke the ice with an apology for weakening the team with manipulation just to see a musician who he found out was into the things he despised. Romella took the queue agreeing she was wrong for not just explaining to Cassy her interest in Drew. She confessed Drew didn't turn out to be what she expected and it wasn't worth breaking up their bond over a guy. Cassy noted her selfishness in thinking she had claims on particular guys while JeLisha apologized for being judgmental because of her own insecurities. DeAndre could clearly see the strengths in everyone and what made the team weak. He explained JeLisha's strengths were how quickly she could see when rules were being broken and her sense of style; Cameron's strengths were his ability to negotiate and find the weaknesses in contracts; Romella's strengths were her networking style and her willingness to be a team player; Cassy's skills were her creativity and zeal; his were to see the big picture and being a peacemaker. He explained the same things that made them strong had also weaken them because of personal motives.

DeAndre summed it all up, "we are five people who have strengths to bring to the group and when we bring these together we are powerful and we live in peace with each other. When one or more of us do something selfish it causes weakness and chaos".

They all promised to help each other stay strong and live in peace as a unit of five and never as one so long as they were dorm mates.

SUMMARY

"*When who we are is over ridden by what we want then what we want becomes who we are*". The person we are can be rewritten by what we want but we can't fully know what we want without facing challenges. YOUR LIFE TEACHES YOU TO LIVE. When we experience enough of life's challenges to define who we want to be then we will know who we really are. We may even change a few times in defining who we are and that's okay because it's a part of the process. It's a great metamorphosis that needs to happen in order to produce an inner beauty that will draw you closer to your desires. The essence of who we are comes from within, when we put Arrogance, Stubbornness, Liberation and Passivity in its proper place as stepping stones to being an Excellent, Strong-Willed, Independent, Humble being; we will have *5 Fingers For A Fist Of Power With Peace.*

There is an attitude we must take on in order to be accepted on our respected levels. We can't always wait for someone's attitude to change toward us, sometimes we must assert ourselves. We have to carry ourselves as if we believe who we are with an expression that says we earned this right because we wanted it.

If you don't believe in what you're doing, no one else will. If you don't believe in who you are, no one else will. *When who we are is over ridden by what we want then what we want becomes who we are.* People can see your potential but won't give you the honor due to you unless you prove to them that you have a standard for yourself. You will be tested on what you say you believe so make sure you really believe in what you say.

It is a normal part of our nature to want to produce replicas of ourselves.....we all want to be immortalized to a degree...we want to reproduce at least the qualities of ourselves that we consider to be good. When we force or manipulate people into thinking or acting like us then we rob them of their independence and block them of the possibility of experiencing the liberation of being all they can be.

It is quite possible to be strong and silent but not possible to be passive and respected. It is possible to be assertive with your standards in a humble manner. How we carry ourselves is as powerful as what we say. We can be a person of very few words, yet be respected. Humility is about honoring yourself without the need for demanding attention for your accomplishments.

The power that comes from grasping all five concepts as a whole is peace. It won't stop life's challenges nor will all problems disappear but I hope it will keep you believing in what matters to you. By trying these concepts, I hope you build a resilience to keep you from giving up your desires. If you use them as your fist of determination to draw from in difficult times, I believe you will prevail with power and peace.

CONCLUSION

There are consequences for every decision we make, there's a reaction to every action and a shift in the relationships closest to us. Consequences of bad decisions can alienate you from good connections while rewards of good decisions will move you in a position for greater decisions. The reaction to your actions is inevitable but some movement verses no movement keeps the hope of your desires alive. The shifting of relationships supports your upward mobility. Relationships that fall away because of your drive to have a simplistic but productive life are like the pruning of a tree. Pruning is necessary for sturdy growth in yourself because it makes room for those independent people to attach themselves to you.

All these things can work together for your good,
For those who *Need To Desire*,
Find the *Excellence Of Arrogance*,

Understand the *Stubborn Life Of The Strong Willed*,
Who push to be *Independently Liberated*
And embrace the *Humbleness of Passivity*.
When you stir these thoughts into a mixture of pure motives you will see that....
YOUR LIFE TEACHES YOU TO LIVE.

I. NEED TO DESIRE

List Your Need Verses Your Desires

EXAMPLE   <u>Need</u>: Transportation   <u>Desire</u>: Mercedes

<u>NEEDS</u>   <u>DESIRES</u>

1.

2.

3.

4.

5.

Will your drive for desires bring you closer or further from those you love the most?

What will you do to make sure you keep those you love and respect apart of your life as you pursue your desires?

Name 3 people you need to stay in your life:

1.

2.

3.

Name 3 people you desire a closer relationship with:

1.

2.

3.

II. THE EXCELLENCE OF ARROGANCE

Write a paragraph on how you can turn arrogance in your life into excellence or a write a paragraph on how you will go about demanding your respect.

III. THE STUBBORN LIFE OF THE STRONG WILLED

What areas are you stubborn in?

1.

2.

3.

How can you turn those stubborn ways into a positive change?

IV. THE INDEPENDENTLY LIBERATED

What are the advantages of having the 3 closest people in your life?

1.

2.

3.

How would your life be affected if each of them left your life?

1.

2.

3.

V. THE HUMBLENESS OF PASSIVITY

1. Are you passive? ___Yes ___ No

If Yes, what experience in your childhood encouraged it?

2. Are you humble? ___ Yes ___ No

If Yes, How do you know your humbleness is not actually passivity?

VI. 5 FINGERS FOR A FIST OF POWER WITH PEACE

What are your five areas of strength?

1.

2.

3.

4.

5.

Have any of these strengths become your weakness?
___ Yes ___ No

If Yes, which ones and how?

References Used:

Wikipedia - http://en.wikipedia.org

Webster Dictionary

Holy Bible - KJV - Proverbs 9:6 and 9:16

Holy Bible - Amplified - Proverbs 16:18

Dictionary.com - http://dictionary.reference.com

Google - www.google.com

ABOUT THE AUTHOR

Doretta Lee enjoyed writing at a very young age. Her 7th grade Language Arts teacher noticed a gift in her and encouraged her to be a writer someday. Doretta never thought much of those words until her passion for writing emerged in her early 20's. She began to write her feelings in the form of poetry and tucked them away in a pile of notes and thoughts she considered personal. By mid 30's she felt a need to journal her painful life experiences up to that point as a way to start a healing process so desperately needed. After completing the journal, she believed her experiences could be used to help others. Finally, she began to make sense of many things she experienced realizing she could have made better choices which would have led her around many of those painful experiences. This book is a summary of those lessons.